KU-507-003

CHAPTER 1

SUPER JACK

GREALISH, GREALISH!

Is **JACK GREALISH** your favourite football superstar? The Manchester City winger or midfielder with the **slick moves** and a **hairstyle** to match is an **AWESOME** footballing talent. The **£100 MILLION man** is also England's most expensive player ever.

B55 090 349 9

FOOTBALL SUPERSTARS

GREALISH RULES

ROTH

pleased
eet you.

We hope you
enjoy our book about
Jack Grealish!

I'm **VARbot**
with all the
facts and stats!

This b

The lc
a furth

WELBECK

SIMON   DAN

Rotherham Libraries	
B55 090 349 9	
PETERS	09-May-2023
J920GRE	5.99
CHILD	RTCLS

Dan Green and Simon Mugford have asserted their moral rights to be
identified as the illustrator and author of this Work in accordance with
the Copyright Designs and Patents Act 1988.

All rights reserved. This book is sold subject to the condition that it may
not be reproduced, stored in a retrieval system or transmitted in any form
or by any means, electronic, mechanical, photocopying, recording or
otherwise, without the publisher's prior consent.

Writer: Simon Mugford
Designer and Illustrator: Dan Green
Design Manager: Sam James
Commissioning Editor: Suhel Ahmed
Production: Arlene Alexander

A catalogue record for this book is available from the British Library.

MIX
Paper from
responsible sources
FSC
www.fsc.org   FSC® C171272

Printed in the UK
10 9 8 7 6 5 4 3 2 1

Statistics and records correct as of September 2022

Disclaimer: All names, characters, trademarks, service marks and trade
names referred to herein are the property of their respective owners and
are used solely for identification purposes. This book is a publication
of Welbeck Publishing Group Limited and has not been licensed,
approved, sponsored, or endorsed by any person or entity.

And this book is all about HIM!

7

DRIBBLING

Jack is absolutely awesome at getting past opponents with the ball at his feet.

MOVEMENT

Quick on his feet, he can easily move in and out of tight spaces.

CREATIVITY

He is capable of making unexpected moves to surprise his opponents.

POSSESSION

Once he has the ball, Jack rarely gives it away.

PLAYMAKER

Jack is brilliant at creating chances for himself and his team-mates.

JACK GREALISH IS SIMPLY ONE OF THE FINEST — AND **MOST ENTERTAINING** — ATTACKING PLAYERS IN WORLD FOOTBALL!

GREALISH IN NUMBERS

Jack wears the . . . **NUMBER** **10** shirt at **Manchester City**

He is the . . . **England NUMBER** **7**

213 **APPEARANCES . . .**

32 **GOALS** and . . .

43 **ASSISTS** for **Aston Villa**

1 **Premier League** title (so far)

More than **5 MILLION** followers on Instagram

A **MASSIVE** **£100 MILLION** transfer fee to **Manchester City**

MILLIONS

of adoring fans all over **the world!**

GREALISH I.D

NAME: *Jack Peter Grealish*

NICKNAME: *Super Jack*

DATE OF BIRTH: *10 September 1995*

PLACE OF BIRTH: *Birmingham, England*

HEIGHT: *1.75 m*

POSITION: *Winger / attacking midfielder*

CLUBS: *Aston Villa,
Notts County (on loan),
Manchester City*

NATIONAL TEAM: *England*

LEFT OR RIGHT-FOOTED: *Right*

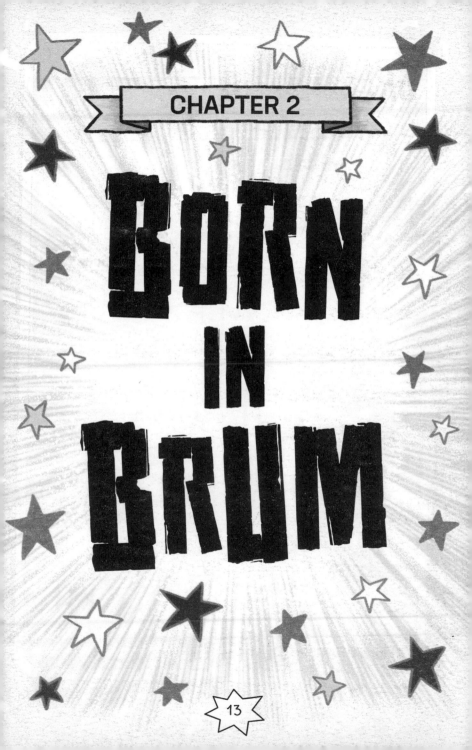

CHAPTER 2

BORN IN BRUM

Jack Grealish was born in **Birmingham**, England in **1995**. He grew up with his family in the nearby town of **Solihull**.

There was his dad, **Kevin.**

His mum, **Karen**

His older brother

Kevan . . .

And his younger sisters, **Holly** and **Kiera.**

Three of Jack's grandparents are from *Ireland*. Jack is very proud of his Irish roots.

15

Birmingham is the **second-biggest city** in Britain. The area around the city is famous for things like . . .

Cars

ZOOM!

Chocolate factories

WONKY WILLY'S CHOCOLATE FACTORY

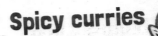
Spicy curries

Heavy metal and reggae music

PASS THE DUTCHIE ON THE LEFT HAND SIDE.

Ozzy Osborne from the mighty Black Sabbath!

Kelvin Grant from reggae legends, Musical Youth.

CHUGGA! CHUGGA! CHUGGA!

And canals.

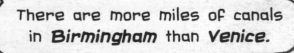

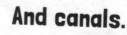

There are more miles of canals in *Birmingham* than *Venice*.

Since he was very little - only **two** or **three** years old - all Jack wanted to do was kick a ball. And that's what he did . . .

In the **school playground** . . .

In the **park** . . .

And in the **back garden.**

NICE, *JUST LIKE* **BECKHAM!**

Wherever Jack, his brother and their cousins

could play football, they would.

SLURP!

Jack was **five** when he started playing at his local football club, **Highgate United.**

Little Jack

Playing in a shirt that was **too big** for him, young Jack was the best kid in the team.

He **flew past** the other boys with the ball almost **stuck to his feet** - and a smile on his face!

CHAPTER 3

UP THE VILLA

Jack's family are **massive** football fans
and they all support the same club . . .

Jack's **great-great grandfather** was the Aston Villa striker **Billy Garraty.** Way back in 1905, he was man of the match as Villa lifted the **FA Cup!**

FA CUP – 1905

Villa beat Newcastle United 2-0.

Aston Villa formed in **1874** – they are one of the **oldest clubs** in England.

Villa won the **First Division** (the old version of the **Premier League**) seven times.

In **1982,** they lifted the **European Cup** (the old Champions League) – an incredible achievement!

Their biggest rivals are *Birmingham City.*

WE DON'T TALK ABOUT THEM!

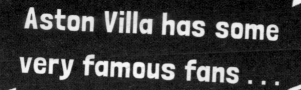

Aston Villa has some very famous fans . . .

Prince William

ONE SAYS, UP THE VILLA. **YAR, YAR, YAR!**

Hollywood superstar, **Tom Hanks**

GO *SOCCERMEN!*

Of course, Jack was a **BIG** fan of Aston Villa himself.

Growing up, his biggest heroes were Villa stars **Stiliyan Petrov** and striker **Gabby Agbonlahor.**

GABBY AGBONLAHOR

ASTON VILLA

And later, he got to play with Agbonlahor!

One Sunday morning, when Jack was **six years old,** he was playing his usual **six-a-side** game for Highgate United.

An Aston Villa **talent scout** was watching.

After the match, he asked Jack's mum,

YOUR LAD IS SOMETHING SPECIAL. WOULD HE LIKE TO JOIN THE **ACADEMY AT VILLA?**

YES. **YES PLEASE!**

THAT WAS IT. **JACK WAS OFF!**

"HE GOT THE BALL FROM THE GOALKEEPER, RAN THE LENGTH OF THE PITCH AND – GOAL! HE WAS THE BEST ALL-ROUNDER I'VE SEEN. EXCEPTIONAL."

Jim Thomas, Aston Villa scout

32

For Jack, playing at the Villa academy was a **dream come true.**

The club knew he was **special.** Jack often played against boys in the older age groups – and they couldn't get near him!

His dad drove him to training **three times** a week after school. It was hard work but Jack lived and breathed football.

Jack's Irish roots led him to another sport as a teenager - **Gaelic football.**

In **Gaelic football** players kick, throw, carry and bounce the ball into a goal or over it.

It's a tough game and the tackles can be *HARD.*

Playing Gaelic football probably helped Jack become a better footballer. Moving swiftly around the pitch, **twisting, turning** and **avoiding tackles** are all part of his game.

Because of his family roots, Jack could have chosen to play for **England** or the **Republic of Ireland.**

Several Villa players played for Ireland, so Jack did too! He represented his grandparents' country at **under-17, under-18** and **under-21** level.

YOUNG JACK WITH IRELAND

LEVEL	GAMES	GOALS	ASSISTS
UNDER 17	5	3	-
UNDER 18	6	2	-
UNDER 21	6	1	-

When the **England** call came,

Jack decided to **switch!**

THANKS JACK!

in **2012,** when he was 16, Jack's hard work in the academy earned him a surprise call-up to the **first team squad** for a **Premier League** match with **Chelsea.**

Jack was an unused substitute, but the chance to train with the first-team was priceless.

A year later, Jack, with the Villa **under-19s**, won the **NextGen** series – a European club tournament.

"BOTH MY MUM AND DAD HAVE BEEN THE GREATEST INFLUENCES ON WHERE I AM NOW."

Jack Grealish

42

In 2013, aged 17, Jack went on loan to **League One** side **Notts County.**

His first goal came against **Gillingham.** And what a goal it was, sweeping through four defenders and firing home. **BOOM!**

NICE ONE SON!

THANKS DAD!

He ran to the stand to hug his dad!

Notts County won **3-1.**

League One football is often tough and very physical. And Notts County spent the season in a relegation battle.

JACK WOULD LEARN A LOT!

NOTTS COUNTY HIGHLIGHTS

The best bits of Jack's loan with **The Magpies**

14 DECEMBER 2013

LEAGUE ONE

**COLCHESTER UNITED 0
NOTTS COUNTY 4**

*More skills in the box saw Jack score the **first goal** and provide an assist for the fourth.*

14 JANUARY 2014

LEAGUE ONE

NOTTS COUNTY 3-0 BRADFORD CITY

*Jack sealed the win with a late assist and a goal in stoppage time. **BAM!***

26 APRIL 2014

LEAGUE ONE

OLDHAM ATHLETIC 1-1 NOTTS COUNTY

The Magpies *needed a point to avoid the drop – and they did – thanks to a second-half penalty.*

Jack was worshipped as a hero – his **FIVE** goals and **SEVEN** assists that season helped save the club from relegation.

47

"I NEVER THOUGHT I'D SEE ANYBODY LIKE HIM, BUT JACK IS DIFFERENT . . . HE WAS UNPLAYABLE . . . HE SINGLE-HANDEDLY WON GAMES FOR US."

Shaun Derry, Jack's manager at Notts County

48

Jack is known for his **looks and style** as much as his skills on the pitch.

Especially his hair - it's all about the hair!

Undercut

Floppy locks

Highlights

Ta-da!

On the pitch, Jack sports a **distinctive look,** too.

He wears his **socks down low,** with tiny **child-sized shinpads.**

Jack has been the **cover star** on **fashion** and **football magazines.**

And he's often on the back - **and front** - pages of the newspapers.

52

He has an endorsement deal with the fancy fashion label **Gucci** . . .

. . . and **Nike boots.**

STYLE ICONS

Jack is not the first footballer known for his midfield flair and fancy hair.

GEORGE BEST

With his long hair, cool clothes and pop star pals, Best was the original fashionable footballer. The Manchester United legend was also one of best players, ever.

DAVID BECKHAM

Famous for his hairstyles, fashions and the magical ability to bend the ball from a free-kick, Beckham is a footballing icon, full stop.

DAVID GINOLA

The smooth Frenchman with the flowing locks lit up the Premier League in the 1990s with his sublime skills. He also advertised shampoo!

I'M WORTH IT!

ANDREA PIRLO

The bearded, long-haired Italian made his name as a midfield maestro at AC Milan. He also looked **VERY** cool in a suit.

"I'D MUCH RATHER BE IN THE LIST OF THE TOP 10 MOST HANDSOME PLAYERS THAN THE TOP 10 UGLIEST."

Jack Grealish

56

Jack returned to Villa for the **2014–15** season after his loan spell at Notts County. He was back with a team that included . . .

. . . boyhood hero **Gabby Agbonlahor**

. . . Belgian strike ace

Christian Benteke

. . . and England midfielder

Fabian Delph.

But unfortunately for Jack and his team-mates, Aston Villa were in **financial trouble.**

The owners had put the club up for **sale** and results were poor.

In the 2014-15 Premier League season, Villa scored just **12 goals** in the first **25 games.**

That's the worst record in Premier League history.

Facing a relegation battle, manager **Paul Lambert** was fired and replaced with **Tim Sherwood.**

ASTON VILLA

HI!

While they struggled in the Premier League, Villa somehow managed a **superb run** in the **FA Cup.**

7 MARCH 2015

FA CUP SIXTH ROUND

ASTON VILLA 2

WEST BROMWICH ALBION 0

*The West Midlands derby. Jack came on as a sub and quickly provided an **assist** for the second goal, but then got a second yellow for diving and was sent off. **Naughty Jack!***

19 APRIL 2015

FA CUP SEMI-FINAL

ASTON VILLA 2-1 LIVERPOOL

*Jack bagged another assist – this one for Fabian Delph's winner that sent Villa to Wembley. **Amazing!***

Villa manager **Steven Gerrard** played in that semi-final for Liverpool.

Unfortunately, **Arsenal** were **too strong** for Villa in the **final,** winning the match 4-0.

But Villa managed to avoid relegation – **just.**

2014–15	Played	Won	Drawn	Lost	Points
17 **Aston Villa**	38	10	8	20	**38**
18 **Hull City** (R)	38	8	11	19	**35**
19 **Burnley** (R)	38	7	12	19	**33**
20 **QPR** (R)	38	8	6	24	**30**

The **2015–16 season** started well for
Jack as he scored his first goal for Villa - a

brilliant curling shot

against **Leicester.**

But things were not going well.

Managers came

and went . . .

HI!

Remi Garde

The club went **19 GAMES** without a win – a record for the club.

The season ended with Aston Villa bottom of the Premier League and **relegated** from the top division for the first time in **29 years.**

2015-16	Played	Won	Drawn	Lost	Points
18 **Newcastle United** (R)	38	9	10	19	**37**
19 **Norwich City** (R)	38	9	7	22	**34**
20 **Aston Villa** (R)	38	3	8	27	**17**

NO!

65

"WE'RE LOOKING TO RETURN TO THE PREMIER LEAGUE. I WILL BE DOING EVERYTHING POSSIBLE TO MAKE THAT A REALITY."

Jack, after signing a new Villa contract in 2016

CHAPTER 8

TROUBLED TIMES

In **2016,** with Villa in the Championship, they had a new owner . . .

Tony Xia

. . . and a new manager . . .

HI!

Roberto di Matteo

HI!

He only lasted **12 games** and was replaced by **Steve Bruce**.

Meanwhile, Jack was getting himself into **trouble,** on and off the pitch.

2017-18

In a pre-season match against **Watford** in 2017, Jack suffered a serious kidney injury after a collision.

He used the time out to think and he focussed on becoming a better player.

He got fitter, trained harder and had a better season, scoring **THREE GOALS** and recording **SIX ASSISTS**.

Jack's form helped Villa reach the
Championship Play-off final.

Fulham ran out 1-0 winners and Villa were
denied a return to the **Premier League.**

Jack **ALMOST** scored
a wonder goal!

CHAPTER 9

CAPTAIN JACK

Villa's third season in the Championship started off well but a run of poor results meant **YET ANOTHER** change of manager.

Dean Smith
(Villa fan)

HI!

But Jack was finding some form . . .

2 NOVEMBER 2018

CHAMPIONSHIP

ASTON VILLA 2-0 BOLTON WANDERERS

*With four minutes on the clock, Jack had the ball in the net - **BOOM!** Then he added an assist for the second.*

25 NOVEMBER 2018

CHAMPIONSHIP

ASTON VILLA 4-2 BIRMINGHAM CITY

*The **Second City Derby** is as big as it gets for a Villa fan like Jack. And he headed in the second of Villa's four goals in this thriller. **HERO.***

75

Just before Christmas 2018, Jack suffered a shin injury and was out for almost **THREE MONTHS.**

DISASTER!

But when Jack came back, the manager Dean Smith made him **captain** . . .

What an **honour** for the lifelong Villa fan!

Jack - and his family - could not have been **prouder.**

GOALDEN WONDER

2 MARCH 2019

CHAMPIONSHIP

ASTON VILLA 4-0 DERBY COUNTY

This was Jack's first game as captain. Villa were **13TH** in the league and playing at home against promotion-chasing **Derby County**.

Villa had scored inside **TEN** minutes and were 3-0 up when Jack got on the end of a corner and – **VOLLEYED** beautifully into the top-left corner.

COOL HEADS

10 MARCH 2019

CHAMPIONSHIP

BIRMINGHAM CITY 0-1 ASTON VILLA

In this **SECOND CITY DERBY** things got out of hand. A Birmingham City 'fan' ran onto the pitch and hit Jack in the back of the head.

The younger Jack might have reacted differently. But now he was the responsible **CLUB CAPTAIN.**

He stayed calm and gave the **BEST** possible reply - scoring the only goal to defeat Villa's bitter rivals.

Captain Jack was leading a talented team that kicked on in the second half of the season. It included the likes of . . .

TYRONE MINGS

- the big man at the back

NOW AN ENGLAND INTERNATIONAL

Mings was awesome at *Ipswich Town* — It's true — look it up!

JOHN McGINN

- the master

in midfield

SCOTLAND
INTERNATIONAL

TAMMY ABRAHAM

- exciting young

striker on loan

from Chelsea

NOW IN ITALY WITH ROMA

With Jack as the captain, Villa went on an incredible **TEN–MATCH** winning run that took them to fifth and into the all-important play-offs.

They met **West Midlands** rivals **West Brom** in the two-legged semi-final.

Jack had assists for both goals as Villa won the first leg **2-1**.

Jack scored Villa's third penalty in a **tense shoot-out**. They won - and were off to a **Wembley final** for the second season in a row.

YES!

Jack was the **most-fouled** player in the Championship that season.

WEMBLEY WINNER

2 MARCH 2019

CHAMPIONSHIP PLAY-OFF FINAL

WEMBLEY STADIUM

ASTON VILLA 2-1 DERBY COUNTY

The Championship Play-off final is the most **VALUABLE FOOTBALL MATCH** in the world.

Winning the Play-off final is said to be worth

£170 MILLION!

86

So it was a very **BIG DEAL** when
Jack led his team to victory over
Derby to seal a **TRIUMPHANT**
return to the **Premier League.**

JACK IN THE CHAMPIONSHIP

SEASON	GAMES	GOALS	ASSISTS
2016-17	31	5	5
2017-18	27	3	5
2018-19	31	6	6

"I HAD NO QUALMS MAKING HIM CAPTAIN BECAUSE HE'S A GREAT KID."

Former Aston Villa manager Dean Smith

While Villa were **battling** to get out of the Championship, Jack was fighting for a place in the England squad.

He made his **England under–21** debut against **Portugal** in the Toulon Tournament in **May 2016.** England went on to win the tournament.

Jack scored **twice** in his second match – against Guinea.

In 2017, Jack was selected by England for the

under-21 European Championship.

Unfortunately, he stayed on the bench.

The manager was *Gareth Southgate*

Jack was nearly **25 YEARS OLD** when he finally made his senior England debut in **2020.**

By the time the delayed **EURO 2020** began a year later, England were tipped as one of the favourites to win . . .

I REALLY THINK THE LADS CAN DO IT THIS TIME!

. . . and Jack was one of the most **TALKED ABOUT** players in the squad.

But he was on the bench for the opening match against **Croatia** . . . and a late substitute in a 0-0 draw with **Scotland.**

England **fans**, the **pundits** and the **press** were all calling for Jack to play.

Jack got his first start against the **Czech Republic** - and it was his assist that set up **Raheem Sterling's** winner.

In one of England' biggest games for many years - against old rivals **Germany,** Jack was back on the bench.

He came on in the second half and it was still 0-0. Minutes later, Jack's **midfield moves** led to Sterling's **goal.**

Then he crossed for **Harry Kane** to head home.

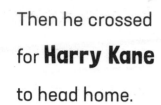

FUMP!

SUPER JACK!

SUPER SUB!

England lost the **EURO 2020** final to Italy, leaving fans disappointed – again.

But Jack was **big news** – a hero and idol to millions.

JACK GREALISH WAS THE PEOPLE'S PLAYER.

JACK'S **ENGLAND** RECORD

GAMES	GOALS	ASSISTS
23	1	6

CHAPTER 11

VILLA LEGEND

2019-20 HIGHLIGHTS

5 OCTOBER 2019

PREMIER LEAGUE

NORWICH CITY 1-5 ASTON VILLA

*This was the **EIGHTH** game of the season and Villa only had one win in the bag. Jack scored the third goal in a **big win.***

100

1 DECEMBER 2019

PREMIER LEAGUE

MANCHESTER UTD 2
ASTON VILLA 2

Old Trafford is never an easy place to visit. Jack **scored** a beauty – and his team came away with a point.

28 JANUARY 2020

LEAGUE CUP SEMI-FINAL 2ND LEG

ASTON VILLA 2-1 LEICESTER CITY (3-2 ag)

*Villa put aside league struggles and enjoyed a great run in the League Cup. Jack's **assist** in this match helped them reach the **final.***

They lost the final 2-1 to **Man City**.

JACK SAVES THE DAY

26 JULY 2020

PREMIER LEAGUE

WEST HAM UNITED 1-1 ASTON VILLA

The last game of the season.

Anything could happen. Villa could win and go down, or lose and stay up.

In the end, **Jack** put them ahead, only for West Ham to equalise. The draw was enough to keep Villa up. Jack was **Man of the Match** and the hero - **again!**

2019-20

	Played	Won	Drawn	Lost	Points
17 **Aston Villa**	38	9	8	21	**35**
18 **Bournemouth** (R)	38	9	7	22	**34**
19 **Watford** (R)	38	8	10	20	**34**
20 **Norwich** (R)	38	5	6	27	**21**

Jack was Villa's top scorer in **2019-20** with **10 goals**.

103

2020-21: JACK'S FINAL SEASON AT VILLA

Jack's Villa side began the season with back-to-back wins over **Sheffield United** and **Fulham.**

Next up were the reigning champions - **Liverpool.** Villa were at home, but there were no fans - it was still the **Coronavirus** pandemic.

Incredibly, Villa were 1-0 up after four minutes thanks to Jack's assist for **Ollie Watkins.**

WHOMP!

Then **SIX** more Villa goals followed, with Jack assisting two more **AND** scoring the final two goals.

VILLA 7–2 LIVERPOOL

*IT WAS AN **UNBELIEVABLE** RESULT, ONE OF THE **BEST** OF JACK'S CAREER.*

JACK'S VILLA RECORD 2011-21

GAMES	GOALS	ASSISTS
213	32	43

By now, Jack was a player that the **big clubs** wanted to sign. Villa would not be able to hold on to their man, but **where would he go?**

CHAPTER 12

£100 MILLION MAN

In the summer of **2021,** after becoming a household name in the EUROs, Jack signed for **MANCHESTER CITY.**

The fee was an astonishing . . .

£100 MILLION!

He was given the **NUMBER 10** shirt.

It was the **RECORD FEE** for a player in Britain.

JACK IS THE **MOST EXPENSIVE ENGLISH** FOOTBALLER IN HISTORY.

BIG MONEY MEN

Jack's **£100 MILLION** move put him among the **TOP TEN** most expensive players of all time. He's in big company. . .

NEYMAR

FEE: £198 MILLION

YEAR: 2017

TRANSFER: BARCELONA TO PSG

KYLIAN MBAPPE

FEE: £163 MILLION

YEAR: 2018

TRANSFER: MONACO TO PSG

ROMELU LUKAKU

FEE: £97.5 MILLION

YEAR: 2021

TRANSFER: INTER MILAN TO CHELSEA

PAUL POGBA

FEE: £89 MILLION

YEAR: 2016

TRANSFER: JUVENTUS TO MAN UTD

Previous British record transfer

Jack joined Manchester City to win **trophies** - they had won the Premier League **SIX TIMES** in **TEN YEARS.**

City have some of the very best players in world football . . .

KEVIN DE BRUYNE

Probably the world's best midfielder in the game today.

ERLING HAALAND

The unstoppable

goalscoring machine.

PHIL FODEN

One of the finest young

players in the world.

RUBEN DIAS

A rock in defence for

City and Portugal.

JACK'S CITY HIGHLIGHTS

In his **first season** at Manchester City, Jack . . .

Scored on his **CHAMPIONS LEAGUE** debut – a 6-3 win over **RB Leipzig**.

Scored against **NORWICH, LEEDS** and **WEST HAM** in the **Premier League**.

Scored against **PETERBOROUGH** and **LIVERPOOL** in the **FA Cup**.

Played against **REAL MADRID** in the **CHAMPIONS LEAGUE** semi-final.

WON his first Premier League medal!

He has played **39 GAMES**, scored **SIX GOALS** and made **FOUR ASSISTS**.

"JUST SWITCH ON THE TV AND WATCH HIM. YOU'LL REALISE HOW GOOD HE IS."

Manchester City manager Pep Guardiola.

116

CHAPTER 13

GREALISH RULES

Jack Grealish has been compared to some of the **GREATEST** players in football . . .

Roy Keane

said he's like

CRISTIANO RONALDO . . .

"HE IS THE STAR MAN, HE MAKES THINGS HAPPEN."

Jack reminds former England captain

Bryan Robson of **PAUL GASCOIGNE . . .**

"GREALISH IS . . . ALWAYS LOOKING TO CREATE. IT'S WHAT GAZZA LOVED DOING."

Jack reminds Villa's

Argentine goalkeeper

Emi Martinez of

LIONEL MESSI . . .

"I JUST SEE MESSI WITH A RIGHT FOOT WHEN HE HAS THE BALL. YOU CAN'T GET THE BALL OFF HIM."

Jack impresses on the pitch with his super moves and silky skills. And he **DAZZLES** his fans off the pitch with his cheek and charm.

As one of the most gifted and loved English players of his generation, we're sure that

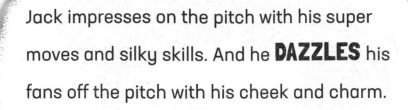

GREALISH RULES!

QUIZ TIME!

How much do you know about JACK GREALISH? Try this quiz to find out, then test your friends!

1. Which city was Jack born in?

_____

2. Which team does Jack support?

_____

3. What do the fans call Jack?

_____

4. What was the first team Jack played for called?

_____

5. Who was Jack great-great grandfather?

_____

6. Which other sport did Jack play when he was a boy?

----

7. Which Villa players were his boyhood idols?

----

8. Who was Jack's manager when Villa were promoted to the Premier League?

----

9. How many goals did Jack score when Villa beat Liverpool 7-2?

----

10. What shirt number does Jack wear at Manchester City?

The answers are on the next page *but no peeking!*

ANSWERS

1. Birmingham

2. Aston Villa!

3. Super Jack

4. Highgate United

5. Billy Garraty

6. Gaelic football

7. Stiliyan Petrov and Gabby Agbonlahor.

8. Dean Smith

9. Two

10. 10

JACK GREALISH:
WORDS YOU SHOULD KNOW

Premier League
The top football league in England.

FA Cup
The top English knockout cup competition.

Champions League
European club competition held every year. The winner is the best team in Europe.

The Championship
The second-tier football league in England

League Cup
The second-tier English knockout cup competition.

HAVE YOU READ ANY OF THESE OTHER BOOKS FROM THE SUPERSTARS SERIES?

FOOTBALL SUPERSTARS

1 FOOTBALL SUPERSTARS
RONALDO RULES
• FACTS • STORIES • STATS
SIMON MUGFORD ★ DAN GREEN

2 FOOTBALL SUPERSTARS
MESSI RULES
GREEN

3 FOOTBALL SUPERSTARS
KANE RULES
• FACTS • STORIES • STATS
SIMON MUGFORD ★ DAN GREEN

4 FOOTBALL SUPERSTARS
MBAPPÉ RULES
• FACTS • STORIES • STATS
SIMON MUGFORD ★ DAN GREEN

5 FOOTBALL SUPERSTARS
STERLING RULES
• FACTS • STORIES • STATS

6 FOOTBALL SUPERSTARS
HAZARD RULES
• FACTS • STORIES • STATS
SIMON MUGFORD ★ DAN GREEN

7 FOOTBALL SUPERSTARS
RASHFORD RULES
• FACTS • STORIES • STATS

8 FOOTBALL SUPERSTARS
VAN DIJK RULES
• FACTS • STORIES • STATS
SIMON MUGFORD ★ DAN GREEN

9 FOOTBALL SUPERSTARS
SALAH RULES
• FACTS • STORIES • STATS
SIMON MUGFORD ★ DAN GREEN

10 FOOTBALL SUPERSTARS
NEYMAR RULES
• FACTS • STORIES • STATS
SIMON MUGFORD ★ DAN GREEN

11 FOOTBALL SUPERSTARS
AGÜERO RULES
• FACTS • STORIES • STATS
SIMON MUGFORD ★ DAN GREEN

12 FOOTBALL SUPERSTARS
POGBA RULES
• FACTS • STORIES • STATS

13 FOOTBALL SUPERSTARS
DE BRUYNE RULES
• FACTS • STORIES • STATS
SIMON MUGFORD ★ DAN GREEN

14 FOOTBALL SUPERSTARS
MANÉ RULES
• FACTS • STORIES • STATS
SIMON MUGFORD ★ DAN GREEN

15 FOOTBALL SUPERSTARS
SOUTHGATE RULES
• FACTS • STORIES • STATS
SIMON MUGFORD ★ DAN GREEN

16 FOOTBALL SUPERSTARS
ZLATAN RULES
• FACTS
• STORIES
• STATS
SIMON MUGFORD ★ DAN GREEN

17 FOOTBALL SUPERSTARS
HAALAND RULES
• FACTS
• STORIES
• STATS
SIMON MUGFORD ★ DAN GREEN

18 FOOTBALL SUPERSTARS
MARTENS RULES
• FACTS
• STORIES
• STATS
SIMON MUGFORD ★ DAN GREEN

19 FOOTBALL SUPERSTARS
BRONZE RULES
• FACTS
• STORIES
• STATS
SIMON MUGFORD ★ DAN GREEN

20 FOOTBALL SUPERSTARS
LEWANDOWSKI RULES
• FACTS
• STORIES
• STATS
SIMON MUGFORD ★ DAN GREEN

21 FOOTBALL SUPERSTARS
GREALISH RULES
• FACTS
• STORIES
• STATS
SIMON MUGFORD ★ DAN GREEN

ALSO AVAILABLE

FOOTBALL SUPERSTARS
FOOTBALL JOKES RULE
SIMON MUGFORD ★ DAN GREEN

FOOTBALL SUPERSTARS
FOOTBALL QUIZZES RULE
SIMON MUGFORD ★ DAN GREEN

COLLECT THEM ALL!

SPORTS SUPERSTARS

1 SPORTS SUPERSTARS
HAMILTON RULES
• FACTS
• STORIES
• STATS
SIMON MUGFORD ★ DAN GREEN

2 SPORTS SUPERSTARS
RADUCANU RULES
• FACTS
• STORIES
• STATS
SIMON MUGFORD ★ DAN GREEN

MORE COMING SOON!

ABOUT THE AUTHORS

Simon's first job was at the Science Museum, making paper aeroplanes and blowing bubbles big enough for your dad to stand in. Since then he's written all sorts of books about the stuff he likes, from dinosaurs and rockets, to llamas, loud music and of course, football. Simon has supported Ipswich Town since they won the FA Cup in 1978 (it's true - look it up) and once sat next to Rio Ferdinand on a train. He lives in Kent with his wife and daughter, a dog and a cat.

Dan has drawn silly pictures since he could hold a crayon. Then he grew up and started making books about stuff like trucks, space, people's jobs, *Doctor Who* and *Star Wars*. Dan remembers Ipswich Town winning the FA Cup but he didn't watch it because he was too busy making a Viking ship out of brown paper. As a result, he knows more about Vikings than football. Dan lives in Suffolk with his wife, son, daughter and a dog that takes him for very long walks.